PRAYING WITH CONFIDENCE

ERROL G. SMITH

DISCIPLESHIP RESOURCES
MATERIALS FOR GROWTH IN CHRISTIAN FAITH AND LIFE

P.O. Box 189 • Nashville, TN 37202 • Phone (615) 340-7285

Unless otherwise indicated, all scripture quotations are taken from the Revised Standard Version of the Holy Bible.

Library of Congress Catalog No. 89-50375

ISBN 0-88177-077-9

PRAYING WITH CONFIDENCE. Copyright © 1989 by Discipleship Resources. All rights reserved. Printed in the United States of America. No part of this book may be reproduced in any manner whatsoever without permission except in the case of brief quotations embodied in critical articles or reviews. For information, address Discipleship Resources Editorial Offices, P. O. Box 840, Nashville, TN 37202.

DR077B

DEDICATED TO

my household saints,
my parents Oscar and Emma Smith:
to my dad, whom I knew for too short a time,
and to my mother who loved me into adulthood
and into the ordained ministry.
Thanks! You still bless me.

Contents

Introduction *vii*

1. I Would Pray if I Only Knew How 1
2. What Prayer Is Not 9
3. Intercession: The Middle Form of Prayer 16
4. Ash Wednesday: The Pause between Words 23
5. Maundy Thursday: Until 26
6. Palm/Passion Sunday: Ride the New Colt 29
7. Easter: The Resurrection Conspiracy 36
8. Praying through the Storms 44
9. Praying Intelligently 52
10. Praying with Confidence 58

Introduction

*I will pray as I am inspired to pray,
but I will also pray intelligently.
(1 Corinthians 14:15, NEB)*

Prayer is mysteriously related to humility. When a person claims to be humble, we know immediately that this person has lost his or her hold on it. The same is true for a person who prays. I have yet to meet the person who is willing to boast about his or her prayer life.

As every Christian knows, there are times when our prayers spill out of us from a depth we cannot fathom. At other times every word, every thought, is measured with meticulous care: weighed, re-weighed, and weighed again.

I have known the dark night of the soul, and I have stretched myself out on the grass to drink from the still waters of God's peace. My prayers sometimes come from a cup, full and overflowing, and at other times they fill an empty cup. I have prayed through my laughter and my tears. God would hear me at both extremes. It is my firm conviction that I can pray about any issue of life. Nothing is off-limits.

This book originated in a series of sermons on prayer. They were first preached as a series throughout the season of Lent 1987 along with several other sermons and homilies for the special days of Lent and Easter. Each was intended to be as practical and as insightful as possible. They are offered in revised form to Bible study and prayer groups so that others would neither despair of their own prayer life, nor falter in their belief in the power of prayer. If this is accomplished, you will be praying intelligently.

The individual reader of this book will find that the chapters are suited to reading one chapter per sitting and then reflecting on the suggested prayer and discussion questions for the chapter. A group study could take several approaches. One chapter could be studied each week for ten weeks, with appropriate time taken for introduction and conclusions to the study. The booklet is also particularly suited to a five- or six-week Lenten study, with particular focus on the chapters aimed at the passion week between Palm Sunday and Easter Sunday.

It would be improper to leave this introduction without placing in print a word of thanks to the people of Faith United Methodist Church for their support of my ministry. They provide this encouragement by their openness in hearing me and through the feedback of their reassuring words that inspire me to return to the preaching task each week with renewed dedication. I am obligated to thank one particular person with a very special word of appreciation and gratitude, Carol Augustino, who entered all the manuscripts on her word processor in a labor of love. She is the one who has made this book possible.

Finally, the most special of all my thanks goes to my wife Joy and our children; Eric and his wife Lisa; Scott; and Jennifer. They have never coveted the time I've needed to work at bringing my sermons to their finished state, and I thank them especially for granting me a week of solitude in January 1987 to go off to the Priest Field Pastoral Center, Middleway, West Virginia, in order to make this series possible.

This effort has strengthened and enriched my own prayer life immeasurably. My hope and prayer is that God will also bless you in the reading of this book by using it to stimulate and enhance your own prayer life. I wish you good reading and good praying.

The Great Fifty Days of Easter 1988
Errol G. Smith

1
I WOULD PRAY IF I ONLY KNEW HOW

He was praying in a certain place, and when he ceased, one of his disciples said, "Lord, teach us to pray, as John taught his disciples." And he said to them, "When you pray, say: Father, hallowed be thy name (Luke 11:1-3).

Each morning when Joe stands before his bathroom mirror to shave he must look over a little card in the corner of the mirror that holds the words of St. Francis' prayer: "Lord, make me an instrument of your peace."

Above the sink in Alice's kitchen there is a shelf. It is uncluttered. "The only shelf in the house that is not a slum," she often says. On it is a slender glass vase with a single flower and a piece of découpage wood on a simple wire tripod. Its wrinkled surface bears the words:

> The air
> the mothering air, the hollows,
>   nests of birds,
> these things remind me always
>   of a God who holds us in herself
>   as in a womb.[1]

Madeleine slips between the sheets of her bed, looks up at the ceiling, then closes her four-year-old eyes as she brings her hands together for prayer and says to God and her parents, "Now I lay me down to sleep, I pray the Lord, my soul to keep."

Jack was never much for going to church. Tonight he finds himself lying in a hospital bed; tomorrow he will have triple bypass surgery. His prayer is mumbled softly into the darkness softened by the glow of the lights in the corridor: "Dear God, I am so scared! Where *is your* promised peace! I'm desperate. Help me get through this, please!"

Someone may have taught these persons prayers to say, but from where did the urge to pray come? Was it God-given? Could it be that the urge these four people felt to pray was also the urge that led the disciples to ask Jesus how to pray? And when he answered he didn't give them a short course on prayer, or a "how to do it" lesson. Jesus didn't answer with principles, or with techniques; not even an outline, but with a sample prayer. It is doubtful whether they felt their request had been answered, but they did remember and record the prayer. That is how the disciples learned to pray, and that is how *we* learn to pray—by hearing and praying sample prayers.

In our technique-conscious world, the disciples' question still sounds timely. Bookstores are loaded with "how-to" books: how to improve your personality, how to make more money, and how to assert yourself. Even so, many persons wish they knew how to pray—so they say. Their defense for not having done much or any praying up to this point is in the confession, "I would pray if I only knew how."

As you move through this chapter, you will realize that much of what you are reading is not new. You will be thinking to yourself, "I already knew that." And you will be right. Learning to pray is not an attempt to say something new, just as much preaching and teaching isn't new. It is a matter of reminding the church of things we already know but tend to forget or neglect. Consider, then, three conditions ofthe discipline of prayer that are essential to meaningful, fruitful praying.

Praying Takes Time

First, *praying takes time*. Whether we are offering arrow prayers, the sentence prayers we say on the run, the prayers at mealtime, the ones we say before we go to bed, prayers said in desperation, those mouthed in thanksgiving, or the prayers we offer in unhurried contemplation—praying takes time. Matthew tells us that Jesus was led into the wilderness where he fasted for forty days and nights (Matthew 4: 1-11). What do you suppose he did with all that time? Fasting as a spiritual discipline is more than dieting; it is giving up eating in order to use mealtimes for prayer and meditation as well as to bring the body into submission. The forty-day period Jesus spent in the wilderness was a retreat, a prayer marathon. Forty days was and is a long time. In fact the number forty is the Bible's way of referring to "a long time." In other words, Jesus was in the wilderness a long time.

Rather than just chalking up days to attain a record, these forty days had a special quality; they were also qualitative time. They were disciplined time. Jesus used these days for a holy purpose. It was not a time for catching up on his sleep, if he could find some shade, or a lazy time for watching lizards play, or a time for staring at the buzzards circling overhead as they rode a thermal column. Jesus went into the desert with a purpose akin to an old Bedouin saying, "The deeper one goes into the wilderness, the closer one gets to God."

Jesus went into the wilderness to pray. *What* he prayed and *how* he prayed in that desolate place we know nothing about. We do not know if he prayed long prayers or short prayers. On this point the scriptures are silent. If I had been there, I would have prayed short prayers, similar to Thomas Aquinas who came to the conclusion that frequency, not length, is the important measurement in prayer. Then again, maybe Jesus did pray long prayers, totally absorbed in prayer to the point of losing all sense of time and place.

We might also assume that Jesus traveled light on this wilderness retreat. It was a lean time for him. In contrast to his experience, when I went on a personal retreat recently I took enough food to last a week, a salesperson's catalog-sized briefcase full of books, several changes of clothes stuffed into a travel bag, and a portable radio. A payphone was in an adjoining building to my cabin, which made it convenient for me to check in with my family each night. When I felt a need for diversion or that I must catch up on world news, I had immediate access to the world. I could leave my retreat mentality and get back in the traffic of modern life instantaneously. Jesus didn't have these conveniences. Assuredly, they can also be impediments to cultivating the discipline of prayer.

Jesus went into the wilderness to pray. He traveled light. He had no tools, no apparatus. Praying doesn't require props. More than anything else, praying takes time. The famous Quaker, Douglas Steere, reminds us of how little we need when we pray: "In learning to pray, no laboratory is needed but a room, no apparatus but ourselves. The living God is the field of force into which we enter in prayer, and the only really fatal failure is to stop praying and not to begin again."[2]

We already knew that, didn't we? Until we take time to pray, we will not pray. Praying takes time.

Praying Requires Honesty

The second condition is no more complicated than the first; namely, *prayer requires honesty.* On one occasion Jesus told a parable (Luke 18:9-14) about two men, one of whom prayed dishonestly and one who prayed honestly. The two men were human contradictions. The Pharisee, a model citizen and regular synagogue attender, prayed his prayer in the temple in a pompous fashion. His words took the conventional form of prayer while he assumed the posture of one in prayer, lifting his eyes and hands

I Would Pray if I Only Knew How

heavenward. But Jesus said he was really praying to himself. His prayer was dishonest.

The publican, a tax collector by profession, whom the general citizenry loathed, stood off at a distance to say his prayer. He did not presume to approach the Holy of Holies, or even to position himself among the other worshipers. He may have intentionally, self-consciously, placed himself in the shadows. There, against the wall of the temple, he was so unnoticeable that the very architecture of the temple absorbed him into anonymity.

Ashamed to lift his eyes to God in prayer, he bowed his head and thumped his fist against his chest as he mumbled his confession, "God, be merciful to me, a sinner!" Jesus told us that the despicable tax collector is the one made righteous.

"True prayer will always give rise to words."[3] But it is vitally important that these words be honest, whether the words are ours or belong to someone else, whether they are in poetic meter or running narrative, whether they are taken from a book or rise spontaneously from our hearts. It is important that they be spoken honestly.

Honest praying is an action of the Spirit. In this kind of praying we are led "to give utterance to sighs and needs that reside in the deep recesses of our inner being."[4] Thus so, it is all the more important that we guard against allowing our praying to become perfunctory. Whenever praying becomes a routine—at meals, at bedtime, with the opening and closing of church meetings, and even in our worship—we need to be careful that our prayers are honest and as heartfelt as possible.

God must tire of wordy prayers, and pompous prayers, and repetitive prayers. How welcome it must be for God to hear a streamlined prayer like that of the Basque shepherd who always prayed, "Lord, here is John." You can't get any more honest, direct, or simple than that. Praying not only takes time, praying requires honesty.

If we would examine our prayers, we would probably discover that most of them are requests for favors either for ourselves or for others. Though the imbalance is obvious, I would not urge you to cease on that account. These prayers are usually fashioned against the pressure of the clock. Knowing that there are other tasks we need to move to quickly, or having been interrupted by a phone call, a knock at the door, or someone calling for our attention, our prayers are frequently cut short. This reality leaves little time for the third necessary condition: that of *listening*.

Praying Is Also Listening

Listening, serious listening, is the most difficult of all the three conditions of prayer to cultivate and master. Noise is so constant that we have grown fearful of the silence. Listening needs silence. Our wordiness betrays how compulsive and presumptuous we are that God needs to be updated about our personal situation, or the difficulties our friends are experiencing, or the volatility of various world situations. This effort of trying to play teacher to God betrays our weak understanding of God. It also reveals a misconception about prayer. Prayer is not a message from earth to bring God up to date with news both local and national.

The Psalmist's word from God, "Be still, and know that I am God" (Psalm 46:10) was a word for antiquity. It is also a word for us. This familiar verse makes the point that listening is as essential to prayer as speaking. Careful listening, just as thoughtful speaking in prayer, requires attentiveness.

When we pray, we need not use up all our time in speaking words. We should pray until, as a pray-*er*, we are the one who is hearing—hearing what God wills for us. As the mystic Amy Carmichael said, "Do not be afraid of silence in your prayer time. It may be that you are meant to listen, not to speak. So wait before the Lord. Wait in silence."

I Would Pray if I Only Knew How

Praying is never just speaking. Praying is also listening, listening for that voice that alone is the holy and undeniable voice of God. Can you picture Jesus those forty days in the wilderness, talking and mumbling prayers every moment? Surely he must have spent considerable amounts of time listening. So we too should consider how essential listening is to our praying.

The famous Swiss physician and churchman, Paul Tournier, recalled in a moment of reflection how he learned to pray as a Christian. He had attended a meeting where four men spoke. Three were professors, including the famous theologian Emil Brunner. The fourth was an official of the League of Nations, Jan de Bordes. Although all were to speak about church renewal, the three professors turned out to be duds; they dealt in trivialities and the mundane. But the man from the League of Nations talked about meditation. Tournier was fascinated. He asked Jan de Bordes how long he prayed and meditated each day. "It depends," said the man. "I am asking for a precise answer," Tournier said. "Well, on average one hour," he said. "Sometimes more."

Impressed and thinking that if an official of the League of Nations could spend that much time in prayer, he decided he could too. So the next morning Tournier rose early, sat at his desk, laid out his watch, and began to pray. Several times he looked at his watch. When the hour was finally up, he realized he had heard nothing. He picked up his watch and was about to get up, when he thought, "I must persevere." The very thought, he said, made him think that it could have come from God. As he sat there listening for God to speak to him, he discovered that real prayer is listening to God, not talking to God. It is letting God speak to us. It is taking an interest in what God is interested in, not boring God with our interests.[5]

If we fail to pray because we have excused ourselves by saying that we do not know how to pray, we are only deceiving ourselves. The disciples in asking Jesus to teach them to pray were also deceiving themselves or excusing themselves from trying. They knew what we know now, that praying requires just three things: time, honesty, and a listening soul. All three are implied in Jesus' response to the disciples who wanted him to teach them to pray. May we be so inclined and so determined to draw near to the heart of God through Christ because the only way we will ever learn how to pray is through praying.

> God of the spoken Word, God of the written Word, why is it that we think you are primarily a listening God? And with our much speaking, why is it we are so slow to listen? In our desire to pray, we would vow to set aside a special time to pray, and to use that time in honest speaking with you, and then allow for more time to listen attentively for your voice and Word, through Jesus Christ our Lord. Amen.

To think and talk through:

1. Write down and discuss with your group your first recollections of praying. What were some of these bedtime prayers and table graces?

2. Of the three conditions for praying, which one is the most difficult for you?

3. Which condition for praying is the one you need to concentrate on at this point in your spiritual journey?

2
WHAT PRAYER IS NOT

Prayer, with its inherent promise to enhance our lives, strengthen us spiritually, and narrow the distance between us and God, is in danger of being trivialized. The evidence is easy to uncover. There are tapes available that are sold with the promise that these tapes can teach you how to pray with guaranteed results. How presumptuous! There is a book available on how to pray away pounds. How presumptuous! Some people pray for God to help them find parking spaces. How presumptuous!

If life were so simple and praying were equally simple, anyone could telegraph the answers to their prayers. But life is not so simple, and praying is couched in mystery. Paul had a much loftier view of prayer. How hard it is to pray when we find ourselves entangled in the ambiguities of life. This is what Paul addressed in his letter to the Christians at Rome when he said, "Likewise the Spirit helps us in our weakness; for we do not know how to pray as we ought, but the Spirit himself intercedes for us with sighs too deep for words" (Romans 8:26).

Some see everything in stark relief: good and bad, easy or hard. If only everything were that clear, but much of the time life is ambiguous. It has been my experience that I can better handle the ambiguities of life and, yes, the ambiguities of prayer by discovering the paradoxical in them. When our praying becomes a problem for us, it is usually because we are caught in the tension of a paradox. Realizing that a paradox is a truth despite two seemingly contradictory positions, let me invite you to consider three sets of paradoxes that affect us when we pray.

Prayer Is Fun and Not Fun

The first paradoxical set would be this: Prayer is fun and prayer is not fun. From our earliest years, we learned that prayer was a devotional act we approached with a hush and with reverence. To pray, a person was supposed to close the eyes, bow the head in submission to God, and possibly fold one's hands together while speaking softly and reverently. Praying, we were taught, was serious business. And it is. But prayer should also be fun.

There are times when our souls take wing and want to fly, when our voices must sing and shout, and our feet want to dance their joy before God. Even then we can pray, with eyes closed, heads bowed and hands folded, but our words can dance and sing for us. The Psalmist felt like this on a number of occasions but, because his words are liturgical and scriptural, it is easy for us to miss the spirit of what the psalmist was feeling. For example:

Yea, thou dost light my lamp;
>   the Lord my God lightens my darkness.
Yea, by thee I can crush a troop;
>   and by my God I can leap over a wall (Psalm 18:28-29).

Now let me set before you a freewheeling paraphrase of this in modern idiom:

Yes, God, you light up my life,
>   so that I can even find my way in the darkness.
God, you make me feel so virile and strong,
>   that I can do both the high jump and the pole vault.

Do you see it? Can you feel it? The Psalmist has caught the joy and excitement of one who has found joy and strength in God. Here is an erupting of gladness like the joy found in the lyrics of the old Simon and Garfunkel lyric, "Hello lamppost, what'cha doin'?"

In the late '60s and early '70s, the church and world churned through social upheavals while basking in the liturgical renewal which Vatican II brought to Protestantism as well as the Roman church. A variety of prayer books hit the market that were loaded from cover to cover with prayers that were playful, refreshing, and filled with happiness. They carried titles such as: *Tune In*; *Lord, Be With*; *Uncovered Feelings*; and *Pray, Praise and Hooray*. They helped many people move beyond saying "stained glass prayers." See if you can catch the spirit in this one. It is called "Humor."

> Dear God, we are thankful for the gift of humor
>   in everyday life.
> Amid sorrow and sour faces,
>   we welcome moments of joy and sweetness.
> Amid our struttings of pride,
>   we are embarrassed by the banana peels
>   of humility.
> Amid the many tensions of the unknown,
>   we are relieved by the gentleness of quiet
>   laughter.
> Amid the tragedy of falseness and hate,
>   we search for the comedy of truth and love.
> Amid our frequent wanderings from your way,
>   we await the call to do your will. Amen.[6]

To pray that kind of prayer is fun. It expresses the satisfaction and the elation of those who live life joyfully. Praying can be fun.

But praying is also not fun. Sometimes it is very difficult. We can't pray the fun prayers when life has us down or stressed out. When we find ourselves rowing against the tide, or when death has knifed its way into our lives, these are not the times for fun prayers. Praying is not always fun.

As we are willing and able to live out this paradox—that praying is fun and it is also not fun—we are overcoming many tendencies to trivialize prayer. This paradoxical approach to our praying is the means by which we prove to the world and make known to God that we take our praying very seriously.

Prayer Changes and Does Not Change God

The second paradoxical set to consider is this: Prayer changes God and prayer does not change God. Here, let us start with the latter phrase: Prayer does not change God. A review of our prayers would quickly provide us a list of examples of what prayer is not and who God is not. The prayers alluded to by Fred Craddock and a few that will follow constitute a case in point that many people who pray to God, do not take seriously that the God to whom they are praying is the great Creator, Redeemer, and Sustainer of the cosmos. The dean of one of our United Methodist seminaries has a list of prayers that are not prayers. She contends that prayer is not an Aladdin's lamp that we rub with our wordiness to get God to do the impossible for us. Nor does prayer summon a genie in a bottle, forcing God to be our servant and slave. Neither is it begging with "pretty please, God" cajolery. And it certainly is not like a letter dictated to a secretary that lists all the chores we desire God to take care of this day. Prayer does not force God's hand. If these are the types of prayers we have been praying, then Paul was right: "We do not know how to pray" (Romans 8:26). How tragic, if like Huckleberry Finn, we give up praying as soon as we discover we didn't get everything for which we asked.

But! Prayer does change God. That truth is attested by the scriptures. God sent Jonah to warn the city of Nineveh of impending judgment, but when the people of Nineveh repented of their sins and hoped for God's mercy, the hand of God's wrath was stayed. When God threatened to destroy the people of Israel because of their gross idolatry, Moses interceded on their behalf and thereby turned away God's fierce anger. Later when God prepared a judgment of fire for the people of Israel, Amos interceded, and "the Lord repented" of the decision to punish the chosen people (Amos 7:1-6).[7]

As the late Harry Emerson Fosdick observed, prayer cannot change God's intention but it does change God's action because God has a different set of circumstances with which to work. Or as another has argued, prayer cannot change God's purpose, but prayer can release it.[8]

Praying does not change God, if it is trivialized prayer, but if it is a prayer borne up by the Spirit, prayer does change God and it also changes us.

Prayer Is Easy and Hard

In addition to prayer being fun and not fun, changing God and not changing God, prayer is easy and prayer is not easy. Every one of us has had one of those moments when we literally fell into prayer.

> The odd silence you fall into when something very beautiful is happening or something very good or very bad. The ah-h-h-h! that sometimes floats up out of you as out of a Fourth of July crowd when the skyrocket bursts over the water. The stammer of pain at somebody else's pain. The stammer of joy at somebody else's joy; whatever words or sounds you use for sighing over your own life. These are all prayers in their way. These are all spoken not just to yourself but to something even more familiar than yourself and even more strange than the world.[9]

That's how easy, how spontaneously it happens. It pours out of us, a predictable reaction of our soul to life. And these prayers are, in addition to their spontaneity, exceptionally honest prayers. Their instantaneous quality does not permit pretense, arrogance, or false piety. They just flow. They erupt. They cascade out of us. The inner springs of our life gush a torrent of emotions, concerns, pleadings, and exclamations.

Then again praying can be hard—very hard. A couple of years ago a man took up a temporary sabbatical residence in the Abbey of San Georgio Maggiore which is located on an island in the bay outside of Venice, Italy. He is a layman, not a cleric. He is also not a traditional believer. He is a noted surgeon who has combined the two unlikely disciplines of teaching plastic surgery and literature at Yale University. After a couple of weeks he found himself one evening in the darkened chapel of the monastery. In the darkness he came upon a figure kneeling in prayer; it was Vittorio, the novice master. The surgeon watched the man at prayer as though through a keyhole. The man's mouth moved in a continuous whisper but not loud enough for his listener to make any sense of the words that flowed. The words were like pebbles worn smooth by rubbing. As he prayed, Vittorio's body trembled and shook as though he were feverish or on drugs or on the verge of a seizure. At last Vittorio crossed himself, rose from kneeling, and sat next to the doctor. Only then did the doctor notice the tears on the man's cheek. Vittorio smiled, relaxed now, unself-consciously—his face still moist. His teeth were white as peeled almonds. "But you were crying," the doctor observed. The monk replied, "It was not grief." "What then?" the doctor said, searching for a reason. "It was the hard work of praying," came the insightful answer.[10]

So few, too few, take prayer seriously enough that it becomes hard work. This prayer is the kind that goes down into the deep abyss of the human soul to strive with God. In such prayers an abbey is no longer an abbey, a church is no longer a church, a hospital room is no longer a hospital room, a dinner table is no longer a dinner table—but each becomes a corner of heaven. At each point the kingdom has arrived. Can there be any question but that prayer is easy and prayer is hard?

What Prayer Is Not

So we might shout back across the centuries, "Yes, Paul, sainted Pharisee turned Christian, we do not know how to pray." But we are trying. We are trying to move beyond trivialized prayer by living through these several paradoxes:

> That prayer is fun and it is not fun;
> that prayer doesn't change God and it does change God;
> that prayer is easy and it is not easy.

So may we pray until all things become clearer, until we understand what Paul meant when he put pen to papyrus scroll and wrote that "the Spirit helps us in our weakness; for we do not know how to pray as we ought, but the Spirit himself intercedes for us with sighs too deep for words" (Romans 8:26).

> Lord, we do not know how to pray as we ought. Teach us how to pray so that our prayers are not trivial pursuits but are born out of earnestness, and deep sighing, and the bonds of our discipleship with you in Christ. Lord, continue to teach us how to pray; we ask carefully and intentionally in Jesus' name. Amen.

To think and talk through:

1. What is the most puzzling aspect of praying with which you struggle?

2. Does thinking and talking about the paradoxes of praying create problems for you or resolve them?

3. Have you experienced in your own praying that point where the Spirit has interceded for you "with sighs too deep for words"? Describe this rejoicing and share with your group.

3
INTERCESSION: THE MIDDLE FORM OF PRAYER

Is any one among you suffering? Let him pray. Is any cheerful? Let him sing praise. Is any among you sick? Let him call for the elders of the church, and let them pray over him, anointing him with oil in the name of the Lord; and the prayer of faith will save the sick man, and the Lord will raise him up; and if he has committed sins, he will be forgiven. Therefore confess your sins one to another, and pray for one another, that you may be healed. The prayer of a righteous man has great power in its effects (James 5:13-16).

In any size church, one can easily discover prayer groups, prayer chains, dial-a-prayer services, healing services, and other means by which persons in prayer are interceding for others. This activity is engaged with the conviction that intercessory prayer is a way of touching God and touching designated people with the power and light of God's love and strength. Our intercessory prayer connects other persons with God.

Intercessory prayer is uniquely different from other prayers, especially liturgical prayers such as invocations, collects, prayers of adoration, and thanksgiving. Intercessory prayer "includes the added dimension of love for neighbor."[11] Sometimes it is love for a spouse as well as a neighbor, a parent or a child, a close friend or a stranger miles away, sometimes even an enemy. Lancelot Andrewes, a bishop of the Church of England who lived 450 years ago, suggested that there were three levels of prayer:

Intercession: The Middle Form of Prayer

- low prayer—where a person prays for his or her own needs, asking God to do something *through* him or her, and not *for* him or her;
- middle prayer—which is intercessory prayer;
- high prayer—where the pray-er adores God and loves God for the sake of God alone.

Praying for others or praying in intercession for others is the middle form of prayer.

There is something about intercessory prayer that perplexes us. It is the uncomfortable note of dependency upon another for strength. We are not only the people who populate the land of the free and the home of the brave, but we are also a people who cherish individuality, boast of it, and protect it tenaciously. It is not unusual to come across people who speak of themselves and their success in life as self-made. Who among us doesn't want to be self-sufficient and independent? Regardless of our credit-card consumerism, we don't like to be obligated to individuals for favors.

Included in our self-sufficiency is the inclination toward detaching ourselves from others. In the lyrics of a song made famous by Frank Sinatra, I chose to live life "my way." But the old sage of a churchman, John Donne, was right: "No man is an island, entire of itself; every man is a piece of the Continent, a part of the main." Each of us is an important part of the family of humankind. Events that occur in seeming isolation can affect people hundreds and sometimes thousands of miles away. Coal-burning power plants without scrubbers in the Midwest of this country and Canada release carbon and acid particles into the air, forming acid rain that plays havoc with the natural conditions of forests and lakes in Canada and northern New England. The accident at the Russian nuclear power plant at Chernobyl spewed radiation into the air making vegetable crops unmarketable and unsafe for consumption, as were milk and other dairy products, in other parts of Europe.

Each month, tragedies take place somewhere in the world. A building under construction or a ditch collapses, killing some of the workers and injuring many others. Or a crazed gunman or woman goes on a shooting spree, killing people in a restaurant or a children's classroom. Our lives are networked together. Near instant communication makes the entire nation and world privy to this news, visually and abruptly. These tragic events are startling and traumatic to the injured and equally painful to their families, their co-workers, and neighbors. All of us cringe with this news. We are alarmed. If we have any sensitivity, we too are moved to feel something, maybe even to do something: to pray for them, to send help in the form of money, to think reflectively about the condition of our own lives, to wonder about the fragility of those who were injured and the grief of those who lost a family member or friend. We are connected.

Cain's question is a timeless and universal one which haunts all of us, "Are we our brother's keeper?" "Are we our sister's keeper?" Do we have a responsibility for each other? Are we connected? That is the magnitude of Cain's question. Inside ourselves at a point of holy discernment we know what the answer is because it is implied with the asking of a rhetorical question. Yes, we are our brother's keeper and our sister's keeper. We have a responsibility for each other. Yes, we are connected. We belong to each other. God made it so.

We could help others if we wanted to: our brothers and sisters on the streets of our cities, the hungry in North Africa, the drug-dependent hoping to break free of the habit, the lonely hunting for a friend who can be trusted, the AIDS victim hoping against hope for a cure and something more than condemnation. But it is hard to give help and to care when we ourselves are sick. Here is where James addresses us.

> Is anyone among you suffering? Let them pray. Is any cheerful? Let him sing praise. Is any among you sick? Let him call

Intercession: The Middle Form of Prayer

for the elders of the church, and let them pray over him (James 5:13-14).

This is the good news, the gospel. James is writing out a prescription for handling sickness and success. When we are sick, we should pray about it. We should take our medicine but pray too that we might be healed wholly. And when we are healthy and happy, we should sing praise to God. Singing is an excellent means of praying our praise. St. Augustine said, "Whoever sings, prays twice." James advises us to pray twice by singing our prayers of praise. And if in our sickness we weary of praying for ourselves, then call for the folks from the church to come and pray for our needs. Tell them, "I need your prayers."

Illness tends to make all of us self-centered and dependent. In our feverishness, our hurting, our inability to function at full strength, we easily become self-centered. We get into ourselves. We are captives within our own bodies. This concern for ourselves can easily degenerate into self-pity. When we are very ill, it takes most of our strength just to be present with others and to maintain the simplest of social and personal functions. Trying to keep one's self going can use up all our strength, leaving few resources to offer to others. Nothing could be farther from our minds when we are weak than trying to be selfless and self-giving like a Gandhi, a Schweitzer, or a Mother Teresa.

Though it is hard and seemingly impossible to help others when we are weak, herein lies the secret to our healing. Human interest stories prove to us that those who rise above their handicaps, illnesses, and infirmities are those who refuse to let their problems drag them down. They *choose* to rise above them. They *choose* to bless rather than complain. They *choose* to be senders of care, rather than receivers. They *choose* to be givers, rather than takers in the marketplace of life.

Intercessory prayer is one glorious way God has provided us for getting away from our self-pity by caring for others. In his classic devotional book, *A Serious Call to a Devout and Holy Life,* William Law wrote: "There is nothing that makes us love a [person] so much as praying for [him or her]." We don't know why it works as it does, but it does. Praying for others and caring for others gives us less and less time to pity ourselves, to brood about our situation, to bog down in unhealthy self-concern. This form of prayer is by nature an act of giving. It is a fulfilling of Jesus' word that whoever would lose his/her life for Jesus' sake will find it. There is a special gratification that comes in caring genuinely for another. Praying for another—the middle form of prayer—is a profound and effective means of caring for another.

It is also difficult to explain to another the peace and deep satisfaction that come over a person when it is known that someone or several people are praying for us. In World War II Germany, Pastor Martin Niemoeller was arrested as a part of the underground resisting church. On one of his father's visits to him in a concentration camp, his father left this word with him before closing their visit: "My dear boy, there is one thing yet I want to tell you, because it will give you joy. The Eskimos in Northern Canada and the Rataks in Java send their greetings and are praying for you." What a word of assurance that must have been to Pastor Niemoeller. He was being remembered before God. People of great spiritual strength and sensitivity were praying for him. What strength that gives and fosters in the soul of a person: you are being remembered before God.

That same sense of power and of inner confidence can be known in praying for another as well as knowing you are in another's prayers. A YMCA officer living in China had a daughter who was suffering from extreme emotionalism. The man and his wife were at a loss because no resources seemed available to help their daughter.

The thought occurred to them to contact a friend who kept a list of persons for whom he prayed every day. They wrote this friend, who responded that it would be impossible for him to pray for their daughter as his list was full. Then he expressed this conviction:

Intercession: The Middle Form of Prayer

"I do not think that I should have more people on my list than I can attend to thoughtfully and prayerfully in the period of the day that is specifically set aside for that purpose. A man must mean business with all the powers of his mind and spirit when he lifts another person in prayer to God. When there is a vacancy on my list, I will include Mary."[12]

This is the testimony of one who believed deeply in the power of prayer, especially intercessory prayer. This is the kind of person I would like to have praying for me. I'm sure this is the kind of person you would like to have praying for you. We stand in awe and admiration of so strong a faith. No wonder James put in his letter: "The prayer of a righteous [person] has great power in its effects" (James 5:16). It surely does. It feeds faith. It engenders hope. It even makes believers out of curious unbelievers.

James did not attempt to explain in his epistle how intercession works. Neither can I attempt to resolve questions about the mechanics and dynamics of intercessory prayer, but it is a most important way we keep faith with God through Christ. It is one of the ways a Christian carries the cross with Jesus in this life. Listen to Alfred Lord Tennyson in "Morte d'Arthur" as he reflects on prayer as binding us to God:

> Pray for my soul. More things are wrought by prayer
> Than this world dreams of. Wherefore, let thy voice
> Rise like a fountain for me night and day.
> For what are men better than sheep or goats
> That nourish a blind life within the brain,
> If, knowing God, they lift not hands of prayer
> Both for themselves and those who call them friend?
> For so the whole round earth is every way
> Bound by gold chains about the feet of God.

As intercessory prayer becomes more and more important for us and more and more natural, we will find ourselves recognizing sign after sign, evidence upon evidence, and assurance upon assurance that "the prayer of a righteous person has great power in its effect."

> O God, we do not understand why and how we are connected to each other by an invisible web, but in our loving and caring for others we sense it. When we pray for another or are prayed for by another, something wonderful and mysterious happens that has to do not only with us and others but You—the creator of the whole human family. Bless us in our praying by helping us to trust that our praying for others does make a difference for them and us because of our faith in Christ. Amen.

To think and talk through:

1. Construct your own ladder of prayer, using Lancelot Andrewes' model. How many rungs will it have and what will you label them?

2. Although many congregations maintain prayer chains and circles, why do you think the church has ignored the urging from the Epistle of James for the elders of the church to come together to "pray over" the sick?

3. Read again the story about the daughter of the YMCA officer. Was the friend's response (that he could not add the daughter to the list) arrogance on his part or did he have a loftier regard for the importance of prayer than most of us?

4
ASH WEDNESDAY: THE PAUSE BETWEEN WORDS

Blow the trumpet in Zion; / sound the alarm on my holy mountain! / Let all the inhabitants of the land tremble, / for the day of the Lord is coming, it is near, / a day of darkness and gloom, / a day of clouds and thick darkness! (Joel 2:1-2).

"Beware of practicing your piety before men in order to be seen by them; for then you will have no reward from your Father who is in heaven. . . . And when you pray, you must not be like the hypocrites; for they love to stand and pray in the synagogues and at the street corners, that they may be seen by men. Truly, I say to you, they have received their reward. But when you pray, go into your room and shut the door and pray to your Father who is in secret; and your Father who sees in secret will reward you" (Matthew 6:1,5-6).

The first day of Lent is a strange day. It is a day of penitence that invites us into a forty-day season of atonement. On this day, the worship of the church addresses our atonement by focusing on our mortality. Can you imagine persons wanting to "celebrate" their mortality, their finitude, their limited life? Personally, I find it strange indeed to be reminded on Ash Wednesday, five days before my fiftieth birthday, that I will die. I know without consulting an actuarial table that I am much closer to my death than I am to my birth. Every morning when I get out of my bed, my body reminds me how far removed I am from my childhood and teenage agility. I don't need a day of ashes to remind me that I am getting older. But I do need a day to remind me that I am a sinner saved by God's grace. We all need a day, many days in fact, to be reminded of that.

Ash Wednesday is such a special day for us, a somber day cast in the mold of Joel's vision 400 years before the time of Jesus' birth. It is designed by the church as "a day of darkness and gloom, a day of clouds and thick darkness." Though the darkness may be missing in the atmosphere of Ash Wednesday, it is meant to be there in our souls, our thinking, our praying. As we examine ourselves before God—examining ourselves for faults, not strengths—we are reminded of how far short we have fallen of our intentions and noble desires.

Appropriately Lent begins slowly and somberly. Parades, balloons, and trumpet fanfares are entirely out of character for this day and this season. In this season we come to God with hesitant steps, much like the household dog who comes to its master with head down and tail between its legs, after being scolded because it did something wrong. So we come to God on this holy day and in to a holy place where we are marked with ashes, to be reminded that we are children of the earth, God's earth. Here, too, we are reminded that the God who gave breath to our fleshy clay at birth will also be there to accept back our last breath.

On Ash Wednesday we pause to sit, to think, to pray. It's an appropriate interlude of quiet and concentrated meditation. Jesus warns, "Beware of practicing your piety to be seen." We listen to these words, knowing that this day is intentionally pious, knowing that it is intentionally symbolic, knowing that it is intentionally somber. Our business here is serious. We keep this day—marking an ordinary day as a holy day in our lives—by using it to drink in God's grace and love. How easily we forget our need to pause from doing all the other things we must do or want to do, in order to be with God and God's people. This day is appropriately a day for silence and, if possible, for only a very few words.

The husband of the popular writer, Madeleine L'Engle, said that

Ash Wednesday: The Pause between Words

the greatest music ever written is the silence between the "Crucifixus and the Resurrexus est" in Bach's Mass in B Minor. Adding to her husband's insight, Madeleine said, "Yes; and I would add that some of the greatest writing mankind has ever produced comes in the caesura, the pause between words. Why are we so afraid of the silence?"[13]

Ash Wednesday is our pause between all our many words, all our many days, for silence, holy silence. We wear a smudge of palm ashes to be reminded of our sin, a smudge made in the form of a cross to remind us that we are forgiven of God and that we belong to God through Christ. We are reminded not only that we shall die, but that because of our Risen Christ, we shall live forever.

> God of the earth and of our lives, the palms we waved almost a year ago have now turned brown with time, and turned to ash in the burning. May the mark of the ashes of this day be a reminder to us that our best efforts at piety are just as corruptible. May we never serve You simply for the benefits and blessings we desire but because You alone are holy and righteous—worthy of our most complete devotion. Amen.

To think and talk through:

1. Check your Bible concordance for references to ashes; usually you will find these in the context of "sackcloth and ashes." Explain the reluctance of people toward public recognition and/or demonstration of penitence.

2. Why are people so afraid of the silence?

3. Is Ash Wednesday observed in your congregation's worship life? If not, would you see value for yourself and others in marking the beginning of Lent in this way? If you do observe it, why do you think it attracts so few people compared to other major observances?

5
MAUNDY THURSDAY: UNTIL

And when the hour came, Jesus sat at table, and the apostles with him. And Jesus said to them, "I have earnestly desired to eat this passover with you before I suffer; for I tell you I shall not eat it until it is fulfilled in the realm of God." And Jesus took a cup, and, having given thanks, said, "Take this, and divide it among yourselves; for I tell you that from now on I shall not drink of the fruit of the vine until the realm of God comes." And Jesus took bread, and, having given thanks, broke it and gave it to them, saying, "This is my body which is given for you. Do this in remembrance of me." And likewise the cup after supper, saying, "This cup which is poured out for you is the new covenant in my blood" (Luke 22:14-20, An Inclusive Language Lectionary, Readings for Year C).

These words above are all too familiar. They are the essence of a very hallowed celebration in the life of the church. Sometimes we need to look for new meaning within the familiar words. Two questions will help an old text come to new life:

- What did it mean for those who lived it?

- And what will it always mean for us who read it thoughtfully?

There among all the words of Luke is a word that hangs like a hinge in history. It is the word *until*.

"I shall not eat it [the meal] again, *until* it is fulfilled in the kingdom of God." And "I shall not drink it [the cup] again, *until* the

Maundy Thursday: Until

kingdom of God comes." To use the word *until* is to talk of time. It says that *now* is important, and that the future will be important because of this *now*.

This notion of time is in keeping with one of the insights in C. S. Lewis' *The Screwtape Letters*. This series of fictitious letters was purportedly written by Uncle Screwtape, an upper management devil, to his nephew Wormwood, who was assigned the task of enticing a Christian away from God. In the fifteenth letter, Screwtape talks of time.

> The humans live in time but our Enemy [God] destines them to eternity. He therefore, I believe, wants them to attend chiefly to two things, to eternity itself, and to that point of time which they call the Present, for the Present is the point at which time touches eternity.[14]

Maundy Thursday is that present moment when God's eternity touches our time and the kingdom of God is present for us, though temporarily. In theology there is a technical term for what happens in this Eucharist. It is called *anamnesis,* which means a memory or past event that becomes present for us. It is experienced again in the present, for the circumstances have transcended time. So the living Christ is real for us in the sacrament of Holy Communion, present to us. The Eucharist is the other end of the *until* of which Jesus was speaking. And every time the Eucharist is celebrated in the church, God's *until* bridges days, months, years, centuries, cultures, oceans, races, genders, and nationalities so that the kingdom becomes real for us in this means of grace. This conviction has been an experience of the church for two thousand years.

When we celebrate the Lord's Supper, we are not celebrating an opinion. We are there by Christ's invitation to celebrate the Last Supper with its continuing proviso for the feeding of our souls. It is God's "until" that comes to pass for us every time we experience the presence of our saving Lord in the breaking of the bread and the sharing of the cup. Blessed be God's name every time we break the loaf and drink from the cup.

O God, who declares beginnings, who makes them happen, and who brings a closeness that truly completes, we have felt your hand upon us at our beginnings, our endings and also in the in-between-times. Let this time be one of those times when the "until" of time is fulfilled in the "not yet" of our lives. May we know it, claim it, and appropriate its meaning in our life and witness to others in Jesus' name. Amen.

To think and talk through:

1. Your group might celebrate the Eucharist after studying this chapter. If a pastor is not available, you could consider a Love Feast which does not require ordained or certified clergy.

2. Have you made a vow with yourself and God whose fulfillment hinges on an "until"? Is it a way of postponing its fulfillment or a recognition that certain things must be accomplished for the "until" to be satisfied?

6
PALM/PASSION SUNDAY: RIDE THE NEW COLT

And when they drew near to Jerusalem and came to Bethpage, to the Mount of Olives, then Jesus sent two disciples, saying to them, "Go into the village opposite you, and immediately you will find an ass tied, and a colt with her; untie them and bring them to me. If any one says anything to you, you shall say, 'The Lord has need of them,' and he will send them immediately." This took place to fulfil what was spoken by the prophet, saying, "Tell the daughter of Zion, Behold, / your king is coming to you, / humble, and mounted on an ass, / and on a colt, the foal of an ass." The disciples went and did as Jesus had directed them; they brought the ass and the colt, and put their garments on them, and he sat thereon. Most of the crowd spread their garments on the road, and others cut branches from the trees and spread them on the road. And the crowds that went before him and that followed him shouted, "Hosanna to the Son of David! Blessed is he who comes in the name of the Lord! Hosanna in the highest!" And when he entered Jerusalem, all the city was stirred, saying, "Who is this?" And the crowds said, "This is the prophet Jesus from Nazareth of Galilee" (Matthew 21:1-11).

If it had been any other time of the year but Passover, Jesus would not have chosen to ride into town on the foal of an ass. And if it had been any other place than the outskirts of Jerusalem, he would not have chosen to ride the colt, either, but it was Passover season and

Jerusalem loomed before him. Both the place and time were critical to what was about to happen. At any other time of year, or any other place in Israel, this spectacle would have been meaningless. On Jesus' part, it was a purely premeditated happening. The cleansing of the Temple that would soon take place was spontaneous; his public ridicule of the Pharisees was spontaneous; but the ride into Jerusalem was not. It was a calculated event.

The ride was staged for Jerusalem, the jewel of the Judean highlands. Jerusalem was the holy city to which Jewish pilgrims flocked three times a year to keep faith with tradition and God. It was an unusual city among the cities of the region, flourishing in trade and human vitality. Jerusalem was an enigma, lacking metals or rich ores, or even adequate amounts of water. There was nothing of importance in or near this city but rock. Yet against all these odds this holy city enjoyed a flourishing life.

Jerusalem has always held a strange fascination for Jewish people. It is representative of all Judaism, as both a holy city and the city which killed its prophets: "O Jerusalem, Jerusalem, killing the prophets and stoning those who are sent to you!" (Matthew 23:27). Elie Wiesel wrote of the fascination and the hold this city has on every Jew: "Jerusalem. A name. A secret. For the exiled a prayer. For all others, a promise. Jerusalem: seventeen times destroyed yet never erased. The symbol of survival. Jerusalem: the city which miraculously transforms [a person] into a pilgrim. No one can enter it and go away unchanged."[15] This was the city, a minor city by our standards, nonetheless a city—the city into which Jesus came *riding a new colt, the foal of an ass.*

A Strange Little Animal

Strange little animal, the ass, or you might prefer, donkey. Known for its sturdiness and its obstinacy, it did not stand as tall and majestic as a horse, nor was it fleet and agile as a deer. Neither

Palm/Passion Sunday: Ride the New Colt

did it have the desert endurance of a camel. The ass, used by both the rich and the poor, was the ancient equivalent of a pick-up truck. It could carry a person or it could carry a load. Most of us would assume that the donkey was the poor person's means of transportation and hauling and that the horse was used by the rich. Actually, that was not true. But it was a burden bearer, an assumption reinforced by legends, and even poems, like this one called the "Prayer of the Donkey," which was originally written in the French language and found among a collection of prayer meditations credited to animals.

> O God, who made me
> to trudge along the road
> always,
> to carry heavy loads
> always,
> and to be beaten
> always!
> Give me great courage and gentleness.[16]

We have also assumed that, because this little domesticated beast was capable of carrying extraordinary burdens, it was humiliating to own or ride one. The biblical record shows the contrary to be the case. When Abraham started out that memorable day with his young son Isaac, on his way to making a sacrifice, the scriptures tell us that Abraham took his ass. No, it was not just any donkey, but his own personal one. The language vividly mimics the ownership and love affair many of us have with our automobiles. And after King Saul died, it was his crippled son Mephibosheth who came to King David riding a donkey. And it was upon his own donkey that Solomon, David's son, rode to his anointing as the new king. There is even a Talmudic anecdote of a King Shapur who said to Rabbi Samuel, "Ye maintain that the messiah will come upon an ass; I will rather send him a white horse of mine."

Could it be that none of this makes much sense to us—this not so grand entry? Certainly we are removed from this biblical event by two thousand years and five or six thousand miles and by culture. If great people and not-so-great people rode donkeys, what then could be its great significance? Somehow it was laden with tremendous significance for those disciples and pilgrims who joined in the spectacle of that Sunday. Maybe it was just the pilgrim euphoria of "going up to Jerusalem" at this holy time. Maybe it was the electricity of being a part of a crowd. Maybe it was the special "group building" that worship engenders when people sing folk songs and hymns. Maybe it was because some saw in this dramatic enactment a fulfillment of Zechariah's prophecy.

A Strange Day

When Jesus came riding a new colt, things began to happen: people spread palm branches and clothing to form a carpeted path upon which the little dumb beast could walk. Psalms and prophecy filled the air. Questions and gossip oozed through the crowd. There was a lot of noise, a lot of excitement, and a lot of hope building on this one dramatic ride.

> Tell the daughter of Zion,
> Behold your king is coming to you,
> humble and mounted on an ass,
> and on a colt, the foal of an ass.

One biblical authority insists that "the entrance of Jesus into Jerusalem is a conscious effort to claim power rather than an act of humility in fulfillment of Zechariah's prophecy."[17] That statement and that idea bothers me because Jesus refused to claim power for himself when he was tempted in the wilderness. He just stated who he was and to whom his complete loyalty was given: God. When he fed the crowd on the hillside with loaves and fish, he didn't claim

Palm/Passion Sunday: Ride the New Colt

the power to mobilize them into a large following. When he healed the sick, he didn't insist that they join up with his disciples, but he sent them back to their families and neighborhoods. He stands in sharp contrast to the preachers of the electronic church who have built for themselves multi-million dollar empires.

In this symbolic ride, Jesus obviously was making a statement, but it was not a statement of claiming power. He was saying something new, yet very old. It was a dramatic rendering of previous teachings: "'No one puts a piece of unshrunk cloth on an old garment, for the patch tears away from the garment, and a worse tear is made. Neither is new wine put into old wineskins: if it is, the skins burst, and the wine is spilled, and the skins are destroyed" (Matthew 9:16-17). The new thing happening on that Sunday before Passover was the colt. Jesus was riding a colt that had never been ridden before. Matthew, Mark, and Luke emphasize the newness of the colt.

A Fresh Statement

The new colt is a fresh statement. To be sure, it is tied to the tradition of Jewish faith and life. It is tied to people like Abraham and his ass, and Solomon and his ass. But it is also something new. It is as new as Jesus' understanding and teaching of what the Lord's Messiah would be like. He would not come like Moses, the great law-giver, or like David with his military and kingly power, or by storming the citadels of political power, like Elijah the prophet. Jesus comes in the power of God's love.

Matthew offers us a word from the Lord in quoting Zechariah 9:9, but perhaps he could have chosen the word of Zechariah which said, "Not by might, nor by power, but by my Spirit, says the Lord of hosts (7:6). That is what Jesus was dramatizing in symbolic fashion as he rode into Jerusalem that special day. That is why he was riding the *new* colt, because love is always new: love that is powerful and threatening for all those who refuse to trust love and permit love in their lives, for all those who build their lives on hate, misunderstanding, mistrust, manipulation, and exploitation. To these persons, love is a terrible threat. Jesus is an eternal threat to all who choose not to live in God's love. Consequently, Christians who take their faith seriously are a threat to people who choose not to live in love.

The whole Christian life is a colt upon which we need to ride. Ash Wednesday is the day in the church year when the ride begins. We need the ride and the experience. It is a new colt that declares again and again to the world as did the colt which Jesus rode on Palm Sunday, "Behold, I am doing something new, says your God."

Many of us have been fed by the Cotton Patch Version of the New Testament. We know this treatment of the scriptures as a paraphrase of the Bible in a Southern idiom. The author, Clarence Jordan, lived through the turbulence of the 1950s and 60s, founding Koinonia Farm in Georgia, and thereby experiencing persecution, ostracism, and danger. In the early 1950s, Clarence approached his brother Robert Jordan, later a state senator and justice of the Georgia Supreme Court, and asked him to represent Koinonia Farm legally.

> "Clarence, I can't do that. You know my political aspirations. Why, if I represented you, I might lose my job, my house, everything I've got."
>
> "We might lose everything too, Bob."
>
> "It's different for you."
>
> "Why is it different? I remember, it seems to me, that you and I joined the church the same Sunday, as boys. I expect when we came forward the preacher asked me about the same question he did you. He asked me, 'Do you accept Jesus as your Lord and Savior' and I said, 'Yes.' What did you say?"
>
> "I follow Jesus, Clarence, up to a point."
>
> "Could that point by any chance be—the cross?"
>
> "That's right. I follow him *to* the cross, but not *on* the cross. I'm not getting myself crucified."

Palm/Passion Sunday: Ride the New Colt

"Then I don't believe you're a disciple. You're an admirer of Jesus, but not a disciple of his. I think you ought to go back to the church you belong to and tell them you're an admirer, not a disciple."[18]

That is the risk. Those who ride the new colt always run the risk of being crucified. If it was so for Jesus, why would it be any less true for us? It makes following Jesus a very serious matter to think about and act upon. But it is worth the cost of the ride. Jesus said, "As God has loved me, so have I loved you. Abide [live on] in my love" (John 15:9). But God help us if we forget that to live on in Christ's love also is another way of saying that, as Christians, riding the new colt can be costly as well as eternally rewarding.

Dear God, our faith is a new colt to us. It is capable of carrying us and carrying our burdens, but we would rather have something more sophisticated or more complicated because we have become so civilized. Yet we know that there is nothing more necessary and fundamental to our lives than loving and being loved. Help us to ride the new colt bearing Jesus' love into our Jerusalem, for Jesus' sake and ours. Amen.

To think and talk through:

1. As Jerusalem had a magnetic pull upon the souls of the Jewish people, is there a place that attracts you as powerfully? for similar reasons? Share with the group *what* and *why*.

2. Is there a fresh way of dramatizing in your life and your church the work of Christ? What is that means and what would you be stating if you were to so dramatize it?

3. On a scale from one to ten with admirer being one and disciple number ten, where would you place yourself regarding your relationship and commitment to Christ?

7
EASTER:
THE RESURRECTION CONSPIRACY

Now after the sabbath, toward the dawn of the first day of the week, Mary Magdalene and the other Mary went to see the sepulchre. And behold, there was a great earthquake; for an angel of the Lord descended from heaven and came and rolled back the stone, and sat upon it. His appearance was like lightning, and his raiment white as snow. And for fear of him the guards trembled and became like dead men. But the angel said to the women, "Do not be afraid; for I know that you seek Jesus who was crucified. He is not here; for he has risen, as he said. Come, see the place where he lay. Then go quickly and tell his disciples that he has risen from the dead, and behold, he is going before you to Galilee; there you will see him. Lo, I have told you." So they departed quickly from the tomb with fear and great joy, and ran to tell his disciples. And behold, Jesus met them and said, "Hail!" And they came up and took hold of his feet and worshiped him. Then Jesus said to them, "Do not be afraid; go and tell my brethren to go to Galilee, and there they will see me" (Matthew 28:1-10).

Death is not a laughing matter, and dying is not a joke. Even though we poke fun at death and dying, these experiences are serious matters, and our attempts at humor are our efforts to distance ourselves from it. When the filmmaker, the late Samuel Goldwyn said, "If I could drop dead right now, I'd be the happiest man alive!", he was trying to put as much distance as possible between himself and death. The comic Woody Allen was making the same case when he said, "I'm not afraid to die. I just don't want to be there when it happens." Death is intimidating. We don't want to touch it, and we don't want it to touch us. Though we may challenge it, defy it, and joke about it, we want no part of it. Its terrible finality alienates us.

An older member of one congregation was known affectionately in her community as Miss Ida. She had come home from the hospital after surgery on her wrist and talked of many things, including aging and dying. She made a remark I still remember vividly. "You know, Reverend," she said, "if we had to die more than once, maybe we would get used to it." She might be right. But we don't. We only die once, and we never get used to it.

Every Death Needs an Explanation

We firmly believe, though, that each of us was meant to live a long, full, and productive life. Anything less is an intrusion on God's grand design. Old age is our goal. In the scriptures old age is an enviable goal, a sign of God's blessing. In fact, wisdom and old age are two important prizes that God awards to people, and it is assumed that the former comes with the latter. Job reminds his false comforters that "wisdom is with the aged" (Job 12:12).

But what ought to be, is not what always is. Persons die prematurely, and it is the prematurity of death that magnifies the trauma of the grief experience. Not only is the grief hard to accept, but it is compounded by our search for answers to unanswerable questions.

After Cain murdered his brother Abel, surely his parents begged to know why. When Uriah the Hittite fell needlessly in battle that King David might marry his widow, do you not think that his family asked why? When Job's grown children were crushed under the collapsing house in which they were partying because a fierce wind came blasting in from the desert, Job asked why. And from the family and neighbors of the eighteen people who died when the tower of Siloam fell, questions were addressed to Jesus (Luke 13:4-5).

When a little child dies because a liver transplant can't be found, that death pleads for an explanation. When two pairs of teenagers form a pact to commit suicide and succeed at it, people ask why. Tragic deaths beg for explanations.

No less a tragedy, no less a premature death, the death of Jesus on the cross raises the ultimate questions about the goodness and meaning of life. It also raises questions about the meaning and possible redemptive use by God of this one special death.

Death has its own innate power to make us inquisitive. But it is resurrection and not death that brings us to church on Easter Sunday. Could it be that Easter is a conspiracy by the church to lure us into thinking about our dying because we did not take time on Good Friday? *Conspiracy.* We all know what a conspiracy is: a secret plot to do an unlawful act. And God has done it. God has broken the laws of life and death by introducing resurrection.

The Crucifixion Conspiracy

But before there was a resurrection conspiracy there was a crucifixion conspiracy. Those who contrived it were the Pharisees and the high priests. It is a shame to be so hard on them. If it had not been for the Pharisees, who emerged following the Babylonian captivity, Israel might not have survived as a people of faith. The Pharisees were the people who preserved and perpetuated the tradition of faith in the God of Israel through persecution and during occupation by the Romans. Unfortunately, some Pharisees took their responsibilities too seriously. Their zeal in holding firmly to the faith became a curse upon Israel instead of a blessing. Instead of

Easter: The Resurrection Conspiracy

helping people draw closer to God, some Pharisees made it more difficult.

To look at Jesus in the midst of the Pharisees is a study in contrasts. Some Pharisees made pronouncements with an affected manner of speaking, holding to the strict rendering of the law. Jesus spoke as one with authority. They did not mingle well with the people; Jesus did. They were bound to ritual and law by the chains of a deeply entrenched conviction; Jesus knew the difference between the letter of the law and the spirit of the law.

They accused him of breaking religious laws by healing on the Sabbath, plucking grain on the Sabbath, and not washing his hands at ritually required times. They accused him of being overindulgent in eating and drinking. He called them whitewashed tombs and a brood of vipers (Matthew 23:27,33). Who knows what pushed them over the brink. Perhaps it was the way he was received by Jerusalem on that Palm Sunday, or his violent behavior in cleansing the Temple, or Judas' betrayal. Finally his life ended by his hanging on a killing tree, a cross. And if that was not enough, his tomb was sealed and guarded by Roman soldiers. His opponents took no chances. They knew that he had prophesied that he would rise again in three days.

That was the crucifixion conspiracy. Unfortunately, it is still alive. We still kill our prophets, our holy men and women. We did it in April 1968: Reverend Martin Luther King, Jr. We did it in March 1980: Archbishop Oscar Romero, gunned down as he said mass in a little chapel in San Salvador. We did it in October 1984: Father Jerzy Popieluszko, a Roman Catholic priest in Poland, killed at the hands of the Polish secret police. We still kill our holy people, who are a threat to those who refuse to guarantee basic human rights.

God has provided an alternative, a resurrection conspiracy. It is impossible to guess how or when the disciples recognized that there had been a crucifixion conspiracy. But ever since that Easter miracle, the world has struggled in coming to terms with the resurrection conspiracy.

The Resurrection Conspiracy

Easter was when the conspiracy began. On that day, God put out the word, put out the message to the whole world through the believers. According to Matthew, two women went to the tomb early that morning before sunrise. Graveyards can be eery, scary places in the dark. Matthew says they only came to look at the grave. That was normal. Families frequently go back to the cemetery the next day or a few days after the burial. It is the human way of helping the heart accept what the mind already knows to be true.

Matthew tells us also about an earthquake and an angel of God who rolled the stone away from the face of the tomb. The angel was still there when the women arrived. In fact, the angel may have been waiting for them. The angel said to them: "You have nothing to fear. I know you are looking for Jesus who was crucified. He is not here; he has been raised again, as he said he would be. Come and see the place where he was laid, and then go quickly and tell his disciples" (Matthew 28:5-7, NEB).

The quaking of the earth matched their inner quaking and fear. To calm their inner quaking, they were told not to be afraid. We can understand their fear. They were walking in the new and unknown. God was doing a startling new thing. There was no precedent for what was happening. "If we could die more than once, maybe we would get used to it." And maybe if we experienced resurrection more than once, we would get used to it, too. It's new. It's different. It's the power of God working in Christ.

As the women started on their way, they met someone. This time it was no angel. It was the risen Christ. They knelt before him, put their arms around his ankles, and held him. He was real. That's how

Easter: The Resurrection Conspiracy

they knew he was alive. It was not the tomb that proved it to them. It was meeting the risen Christ.

A pastor in Texas tells this story about himself and his grandson. One morning he was getting dressed. Actually he was tying his shoes, but his mind was a thousand miles away. His grandson, age five, appeared in the upstairs bedroom with a probing question: "Pa Pa, Jesus died for our sins, didn't he?"

Well, this grandfather and pastor wasn't sure where his grandson was coming from. "Yes, David Bruce," he paused, "and three days later God raised Jesus from the dead, and today the spirit of Christ lives in our hearts."

This wee one of God pondered that for a few seconds and came back, "Pa Pa, does Jesus live in my heart?"

"Well, do you love Jesus?"

"Uh huh."

"Then Jesus does live in your heart!" to which the five-year-old uncorked, "All riiiiight!!!"

That is Easter, letting a little child lead us. This is feeling it and knowing it all at once.

Experiencing Easter with this level of assurance and joy makes each of us a part of the conspiracy to turn the world upside down for Christ. Thus principalities, powers, and individuals are threatened by people filled with God's love and peace, especially when they struggle for justice and redemption of all people. And when we face our own deaths, we still hope that we shall live forever. Not merely a hope, it is also a promise given to us from God through Christ.

E. B. White, the essayist, was watching his wife, Katherine, in the late autumn of her life and in the autumn of the year. She was preparing to plant bulbs that would bloom the next spring, flowers she would never live to see. Of her he wrote, "There was something comical yet touching in her bedraggled appearance . . . the small hunched-over figure, her studied absorption in the implausible notion that there would be yet another spring, oblivious to the ending of her own days, which she knew perfectly well was near at hand, sitting there with her detailed chart under those dark skies in dying October, calmly plotting the resurrection."

Of her, someone else said: "Katherine was a member of the resurrection conspiracy, the company of those who plant seeds of hope under dark skies of grief or oppression, going about their living and dying until, no one knows how, when or where, the Easter shoots appear, and a piece of creation is healed."[19]

Each person who bends the knee to Jesus is a member of the resurrection conspiracy. Each person who bows the head to Jesus is a member of the resurrection conspiracy. Each person who is baptized and nicknamed Christian is a member of the resurrection conspiracy. Each person who calls on the name of Jesus in prayer is a member of the resurrection conspiracy.

We are not only citizens of the world, God's world, but also citizens of the kingdom, God's kingdom, because we belong in the resurrection conspiracy. Death no longer has dominion over us. We can joke and laugh at death because it no longer has the sting for us that it has for those without hope. We are going to live with Christ and we are going to live forever. Thanks be to God. Alleluia!

> Dear God, we praise you because Christ is risen! When he is alive in us, we are more alive than when he is not in us. We thank you for giving us life in all its fullness through a risen Lord with whom we share the thrill and satisfaction of being a part of the resurrection conspiracy. Amen.

To think and talk through:

1. The people of the Judeo-Christian tradition have always fostered a Puritan element. Name the virtues of the Pharisees and the Puritans. If necessary, do some research into the history of both.

2. Can you name an experience you have had of God that produced

Easter: The Resurrection Conspiracy

real fear? If not, have you recently had an experience of fear not associated with faith? Can you in retrospect now see a relationship between that fear and your faith?

3. Name some people you know who are living the resurrection conspiracy. Why do you identify them in this way? Why are they so special?

8
PRAYING THROUGH THE STORMS

Then Jesus went with them to a place called Gethsemane, and he said to his disciples, "Sit here, while I go yonder and pray." And taking with him Peter and the two sons of Zebedee, he began to be sorrowful and troubled. Then he said to them, "My soul is very sorrowful, even to death; remain here, and watch with me." And going a little farther he fell on his face and prayed, "My Father, if it be possible, let this cup pass from me; nevertheless, not as I will, but as thou wilt." And he came to the disciples and found them sleeping; and he said to Peter, "So, could you not watch with me one hour? Watch and pray that you may not enter into temptation; the spirit indeed is willing, but the flesh is weak." Again, for the second time, he went away and prayed, "My Father if this cannot pass unless I drink it, thy will be done." And again he came and found them sleeping, for their eyes were heavy. So, leaving them again he went away and prayed for the third time, saying the same words. Then he came to the disciples and said to them, "Are you still sleeping and taking your rest? Behold, the hour is at hand, and the Son of man is betrayed into the hands of sinners. Rise, let us be going; see, my betrayer is at hand" (Matthew 26:36-46).

Bishop Earl Hunt told of an unforgettable person whom he had known most of his life, Miss Mary Culler White. She was, in his words, "a diminutive and indomitable Methodist missionary to

China." He visited her during her final illness when she was 95 years old at a retirement and nursing center in North Carolina. When they were about to conclude the visit, she offered this prayer for the bishop: "Now Lord, thou knowest that Earl has come to see me and thou knowest that he is a bishop. But thou art also aware that this doesn't mean a thing in the world to me!"

Having captured the bishop's attention as well as God's, she proceeded to pray with great thoroughness and with the most tender compassion for every need in his family's life about which she had any knowledge. As she drew her prayer to a close, she declared: "And thou knowest, O God, that in such matters I am not accustomed to being denied!"[20]

Coming from most people, that closing charge to the Lord would have hung in the air as a resounding word of arrogance, if not triteness. But this elderly missionary could pray forcefully and with this level of candor because of her own integrity and deep faith. She and God were personal friends and in that friendship she was claiming the blessed benefits of their relationship. Few of us have that audacity, because few of us have had to follow our Christ through the storms, the terrible storms, which she had known in her lifetime.

Although many are not comfortable in praying publicly, most people do pray with a certain ease. Our prayers arise from our hearts and thoughts in times of great happiness as well as from those times when life gets sticky and sometimes overwhelming. Why is it, though, that praying gets harder when we are undone, when we are devastated by life? When our life feels like a ball of kite string that has come unraveled and lies knotted and tangled about us, praying is harder. When our lives seem out of control, our career is going nowhere, or is going downhill, our marriage is coming unglued, our studies are burying us, our finances are a disaster, our faith is a collection of words without meaning, prayer is not easy. When we are stretched thin, fatigued, short-tempered, desperate for a sense of God's presence and blessing, praying comes harder. This is what I call praying through the storms or what the late Harry Emerson Fosdick called "prayer as battlefield" (*The Meaning of Prayer*).

Praying Unselfishly

If we are going to pray our way through the storms, it would benefit us to begin by praying purely and unselfishly. This approach is only a variation on the theme of an earlier chapter, namely, to pray honestly. In W. H. Auden's *A Christmas Oratorio* there is a most unique prayer. Without a doubt it is a facetious prayer, a tongue-in-cheek prayer, which he wrote deliberately as an exaggerated way of poking fun at our many weak prayers. As you read it, you may realize that your prayers, like many of mine, are trite and beggarly.

> O God, put away justice and truth for we cannot understand them and do not want them. Eternity—would bore us dreadfully. Leave thy heavens and come down to our earth of waterclocks and hedges. Become our uncle. Look after Baby, amuse Grandfather, escort Madam to the opera, help Willy with his homework, introduce Muriel to a handsome naval officer. Be interesting and weak like us, and we will love you as we love ourselves.[21]

When our prayers sound as facetious and humorous as that, we realize that this kind of prayer will not carry us through the storms, nor will it be of any solace or help. Such prayers are worthless and impure, a wasted effort.

Better that we should throw ourselves on the mercy of God. Better that we should admit how helpless and hurt we are. Better we should plead with God as did the Psalmist:

> How long, O Lord? Wilt thou forget me for ever?
> How long wilt thou hide thy face from me?

> How long must I bear pain in my soul,
> and have sorrow in my heart all the day? (Psalm 13:1-2)

This prayer is pure. This prayer is honest with God. Equally honest are three lines from three different stanzas of a modern poem, which resonates more like a psalm.

> I teach my sight to lengthen into songs . . .
> Dark hangs upon the waters of the soul . . .
> A raw ghost drinks the fluid in my spine.[22]

Better we should pray to God with this kind of honesty than to ask that Muriel be introduced to a handsome naval officer. If we are hurting, if we are struggling, or if we are crushed, it is time for us to pray honestly about our personal situation, even if our only words are: "How long, O Lord, how long?"

Hannah's Prayer—A Model Prayer

Assuming that we are able to pray as honestly as the Psalmist and as forthrightly as a poet, we are still faced with the dilemma of deciding what to pray. Is it acceptable to go directly to the heart of the situation and ask for a solution? Can we in good conscience ask for a new job when the old one has collapsed underneath us, a new level of trust from our spouse to restore our marriage when there is no basis for that trust, or an A− or B+ on a paper that is not a passing effort, a few thousand dollars to pay off our charge accounts, or a large sum to put down on a new house? We may find a clue in the Old Testament.

Hannah was a childless woman in a world that considered childlessness a curse, a mark of shame, a sign that one was not in God's favor. She was one of the two wives of Elkanah. The name of the other wife was Peninnah. (It was the custom of that time for a man to have more than one wife.) Peninnah had several children and she taunted her childless sister-wife, Hannah. (This story is told in the first chapter of 1 Samuel.)

Hannah reached the breaking point. She felt that the best way of addressing the problem of her childlessness was to appeal to God. She prayed. It was not a gentle prayer but one that rose out of her anger, frustration, and hopelessness. The Bible says that "in the bitterness of her soul she prayed to Yahweh with many tears" (1 Samuel 1:10, Jerusalem Bible). Without any self-consciousness, she asked for a baby, a boy baby. Having a son would give her respect in the community and in her own family. To give birth to a boy-child would make her feel fulfilled. Others would look at her and see that God had blessed her rather than forsaken her.

The significant difference between Hannah's prayer and many of our own is that her prayer was for much more than a solution. She prayed a good prayer, but she also attached to it a vow. In this vow she made a commitment not only to receive the gift from God but also to give the gift back to God as a blessing.

How many of us pray that kind of prayer? It would be impossible to count the number of people who have made promises to pastors in the hospital and at funeral homes about coming back and taking seriously their participation in the fellowship and worship life of the church. But the odds are that very few have kept these promises after they made it through that hospital experience or their grief, with God's help. These vows that were made were probably well intentioned, or perhaps with the understanding that no one would hold them accountable; that is, the pastor would be too polite, the church too kind, and God too busy.

Few of us spend time analyzing either the content of or the motives behind our prayers; consequently, it is natural that we fail to realize any responsibility for helping God to answer our prayers. If vows were attached to our prayers of supplication and intercession, that would be a giant stride toward recognizing our responsibility for helping the prayer find an answer, inasmuch as that is humanly possible. Of course, prayers of a contemplative character involve a different set of dynamics. The very art of forging a definition for prayer could be a meaningful spiritual exercise for every Christian.

In a book of contemporary prayers, the opening page lists about thirteen or fourteen definitions for prayer. One in particular stands out: A prayer is . . . a bunch of words, often meaningless, offered up to God in hopes that they find meaning.[23] When we offer a prayer and ask for a serious answer or a solution to a very real problem that we are facing, our words, like Hannah's, are meaningless words offered to God until God gives them meaning in that they are heard, our individuality is noted, and the anguish of our soul is felt in God's heart. Hannah spoke out of her grief and resentment, and God recognized her honesty, yes, even the depth of her desire. So we should ask God to help meet our needs even when our words reflect anger, doubt, resentment, anguish, sorrow, or overwhelming unbelief. It is all right, even essential, that we pray for solutions to problems. God expects us to be concrete, specific, and true.

Our Prayer: An Effective Prayer

As we pray concretely, we ought also to pray that God's will be done. This means praying for the wisdom to recognize God's will and the courage to accept it. When Jesus went into the Garden of Gethsemane on the night of his betrayal, Matthew 26:38 tells us that "he began to be sorrowful and troubled." To his three disciples (Peter, James, and John) he said, "My soul is very sorrowful, even to death; remain here, and watch [or, keep awake] with me" (Matthew 26:38). In saying this, Jesus was expecting that they would understand the depth of his own inner struggle and his desire that they pray with him.

Three times he prayed that the inevitable cup of suffering might not need to be drunk. Three times he got up from where he was praying to check on the three disciples only to find them sleeping. Reflecting on this special night, it ought to occur to us that more was involved here than the mere language of prayer, or the hope that he would not have to die, but also the deeper concern of not being abandoned by God. Words of this magnitude would come from his lips the next day as he hung on the cross, "My God, my God, why hast thou forsaken me?" (Matthew 27:46).

Every prayer we pray in our trials and tribulations is essentially a prayer that God will not abandon us at our moment of need. Even if the answer to our prayer for our rescue or help is *not* a matter of deliverance, we at least want God to be near to see us through. "God is a very present help in trouble" is the confession of faith of the Psalmist (Psalm 46:1) and of the church.

Several decades ago, Professor Royce of Harvard University gave this testimony: "When things are too much for me, and I am down on my luck, and everything is dark, I go alone by myself, and I bury my head in my hands. I think hard that God must know it all and will see how matters really are, and understand me; and in just that way alone, by understanding me, will help me. And so I try to get myself together, and that, for me, is prayer."[24]

Placing one's self in God's will is that toward which we walk, crawl, or run as we pray our way through the storms. Though troubled, even to death, it is our intense prayer that God will not abandon us, because that is ultimate desolation. Mother Teresa reminds us of that in her work among the poorest of the poor. "What the poor need even more than food and clothing and shelter (though they need these, too, desperately) is to be wanted. I have come more and more to realize that it is being unwanted that is the worst disease that any human being can ever experience."[25]

Like the prayer Jesus prayed in the garden, the prayer that ultimately thy will be done, should set the tone for the prayers we pray through the storms: prayers that we will not be alone though the winds blow hard, though the waves mount high, and the night be very dark—prayers that the God who created the seas and all that is in them will also calm the storms until we arrive safely at the shores of the land of God's everlasting peace.

> If we should stop praying, especially in the stormy times of our lives, O God, then we have left ourselves alone. May we pray at those times purely, concretely, and with the intent of discovering your will, that we might courageously endure to the end of life, with your blessing on us all our days through Christ. Amen.

To think and talk through:

1. Write your own definition for prayer. Try not to make it sound too churchy.

2. Since the disciples lived so closely with Jesus for three years, why do you think they were so insensitive to the anguish of his praying in the Garden of Gethsemane?

3. Distinguish between a fatalism and relinquishment in Jesus' prayer for "God's will to be done."

9
PRAYING INTELLIGENTLY

I say, then, that the man who falls into ecstatic utterance should pray for the ability to interpret. If I use such language in my prayer, the Spirit in me prays, but my intellect lies fallow. What then? I will pray as I am inspired to pray, but I will also pray intelligently. I will sing hymns as I am inspired to sing, but I will sing intelligently too. Suppose you are praising God in the language of inspiration: how will the plain man who is present be able to say "Amen" to your thanksgiving, when he does not know what you are saying? Your prayer of thanksgiving may be all that could be desired, but it is no help to the other man. Thank God, I am more gifted in ecstatic utterance than any of you, but in the congregation I would rather speak five intelligible words, for the benefit of others as well as myself, than thousands of words in the language of ecstasy (1 Corinthians 14:13-19, NEB).

Finding an agreeable definition for intelligence might be a difficult task. One of our former presidents said, "An intellectual is a person who takes more words than necessary to tell more than they know." Another man said, "If an animal does something, we call it instinct; if we do the same thing for the same reason, we call it intelligence." All of us fear that a world full of intellectuals could be a calamity rather than a great blessing. This sentiment found fine expression at the hands of another who said, "If everybody contemplates the infinite instead of fixing the drains, many of us will die of cholera."

In the popular little book of fiction, *The Screwtape Letters*, a senior devil by the name of Screwtape is tutoring a novice devil by the name of Wormwood. Wormwood has been assigned to a particular victim to seduce him away from the Christian faith. The tutoring is handled by means of letters and memos. Toward the latter part of the series of letters, the male earthling has fallen in love with a woman. Screwtape perceived this change of events as a prime opportunity for temptation. In the fourth of his twenty-seven correspondences, he writes:

> Now that he is in love, a new idea of *earthly* happiness has arisen in his mind: and hence a new urgency in his purely petitionary prayers. Now is the time for raising intellectual difficulties about prayer. False spirituality is always to be encouraged.[26]

Each person has intellectual difficulties with prayer. Even Paul had his questions, yet he wrote to the believers at Corinth, "I will pray as I am inspired to pray, but I will also pray intelligently" (NEB). Paul was stating this intention in the context of praying in understandable words as opposed to the ecstatic language of speaking in tongues (*glossolalia*). Perhaps you will not consider it a rude treatment of the text to take it out of this context slightly to let it address us with another voice for our time.

Language is that fluid flow of words by which we communicate with each other. But language is never static; it is ever-changing. Words that held great weight in one era may not, after a passage of time, register any weight on the scales of our understanding. For example, two phrases from prayers in the service for Holy Communion find less use because of newer liturgies, namely, "creatures of bread and wine" or "manifold and great mercies." *Creatures,* to us, is strongly associated with animals, and *manifold* is more commonly referred to as an important part of the exhaust system of our car. Using words that have stronger meanings fixed in an entirely different context is hardly what Paul would call "praying intelligently," even when they are gilded by time in an older service of the church, and have been polished to a high luster by years of reverent usage.

Praying should make sense. The words we use should be understandable. If we can't make ourselves understood to ourselves and to others, how can we expect God to understand what we are praying? "I will pray as I am inspired to pray, but I will also pray intelligently."

Praying with the Heart

But wait a minute! Something inside us says, "Not so fast!" An argument begins to brew within us. The heart says, "You must pray with the heart and not with the mind." The mystic, Blaise Pascal, says, "the heart has its reasons, which the mind knows not of." And it does. The heart has its own reasons.

We have heard many dull prayers in our lifetime. We have heard prayers that didn't say anything and were sent nowhere. And when we have heard such prayers, devoid of life, passion, emotion, and feeling, something inside us has turned critical and said, "That's not praying; praying is more important. Praying is something else. Prayer has a heart and a pulse."

When we are skimming our way through the Bible, it is not hard to find prayers offered up by people in stressful moments and ecstatic ones. Take the crusty prophet Elijah hiding on top of Mount Horeb. In his despair and loneliness he tells God, "'the people of Israel have forsaken thy covenant . . . and I, even I only, am left; and they seek my life, to take it away'" (1 Kings 19:14). That prayer has feeling. It is filled with pathos. David provides us with another example of passionate praying. When Absalom, his son and rival for the throne was killed in battle, David prayed, "'O my son Absalom, my son, my son Absalom! Would I had died instead of you, O Absalom, my son, my son'" (2 Samuel 18:33)! Do you sense the emotion, the grief?

On the other hand some psalms are a rich treasure chest of praise. Sense the joy: "Clap your hands, all peoples! / Shout to God with loud songs of joy! / For the Lord, the Most High, is terrible, a great king over all the earth" (Psalm 47:1-2); or "Make a joyful noise to God, all the earth; / sing the glory of his name; / give to him glorious praise" (Psalm 66:1)!

When Beethoven had played a new sonata for a friend, the friend asked him after the last note, "What does it mean?" Beethoven returned to the piano, played the whole sonata again and said, "That is what it means."[27] It is equally true of our praying. Praying from the heart needs no justification. Still, Paul's words hang hauntingly in the air like a ghost we cannot escape, "I will pray as I am inspired to pray, but I will also pray intelligently." He will pray with the heart, but he will also pray with his head.

Praying with the Head

Surprisingly you can reverse Blaise Pascal's words and they will continue to ring true: "The mind has its reasons, that the heart knows not of, too." There is a center of questioning in all of our minds. We pray and ask: "How does prayer work? How do we connect with God? Is there a cause-and-effect relationship in our praying?" All of us struggle with these questions. They are not easily answered and possibly only to our partial satisfaction. But there is a reasoning that lies behind the questions themselves. It is our innate desire to make sense of life. It is our struggle against absurdity. Our questions are the way we search for a pattern, a purpose, a rationale to life. If we cannot make sense of life, then life is meaningless, and if meaningless then hopeless.

So our minds spawn questions. Our minds were created by God to ask questions, to solve problems, to figure out life. God not only gave us a conscience but also the ability to understand. The mind is not an ungodly part of us. Praying intelligently and thinking our faith through intelligently may not come as easily, as spontaneously, as the emotional part for some. For others, the emotions come more slowly and are harder to stimulate. Thomas asked Jesus, "'Lord, we do not know where you are going; how can we know the way'" (John 14:5)? Philip asked, "'Lord, show us the Father, and we shall be satisfied'" (John 14:8)? And Pilate asked Jesus, "'Are you the King of the Jews?'" (Matthew 27:11) and "'What is truth?'" (John 18:38) Do you see in these words the mind's hunger to know and to know for sure?

Up to this point, we have been weighing in one hand and then the other whether to pray with the heart or with the head. But this doesn't have to be our choice. In fact, there doesn't have to be a choice. We don't have to choose between alternatives. The wise decision embraces both. Unless and until we pray both with the heart and the head, our prayers will be less than they could be. Our praying, like our theologizing, has to be intellectually respectable; our mind is needed. And our praying, like our theologizing, needs to be conveyed with a passion; it needs to be heartfelt.

It is hard to imagine being a vibrant Christian without being a praying person. Praying, like other spiritual disciplines, needs constantly to be cultivated and deepened. Praying does make sense. It is an intelligent response of our lives to God through Christ. And though it has practical physical effects—praying can produce the benefits of lowering our blood pressure, slowing our pulse rate, and relaxing us physically—there is a wisdom far beyond these effects upon our bodies. It has a spiritual effect upon all of creation. In fact we end up praying more than words; we find ourselves praying our lives. In the novel, *Just Above My Head,* a black singer who is the chief character spills out his philosophy about music and his own

Praying Intelligently

life, saying, "When you sing, you can't sing outside the song. You've got to *be* the song you sing."[28] How easily and truthfully that yields to a paraphrase: "When you pray, you can't pray outside your prayer. You've got to be the prayer you pray." In biblical imagery, this is praying with the heart and praying with the head at the same time. This is surely what Paul meant in using the phrase "praying intelligently."

> O God, you are the only one to whom we pray. When we do it out of habit, or custom, or ritual—failing to breathe feeling and passion into our prayers, please forgive. And when we pray a profusion of words out of great passion but fail to think our way into and through our prayers, robbing them of meaning and direction, please forgive. Help us to balance our passion and our intellect in the effort of our praying until we are able to not only say our prayers but to also live our prayers before you. This we pray in Jesus' name. Amen.

To think and talk through:

1. Why does the church continue to value education and at the same time demean the mind in favor of the heart?

2. Name some points at which you see the continuing struggle occurring between passion and the integrity of the mind in your life or congregation.

3. Are you finding it difficult to be the prayer you have been praying recently? If it is not too confidential a matter, share your struggle with the group.

10
PRAYING WITH CONFIDENCE

And he told them a parable, to the effect that they ought always to pray and not lose heart. He said, "In a certain city there was a judge who neither feared God nor regarded man; and there was a widow in that city who kept coming to him and saying, 'Vindicate me against my adversary.' For a while he refused; but afterward he said to himself, 'Though I neither fear God nor regard man, yet because this widow bothers me, I will vindicate her, or she will wear me out by her continual coming.'" And the Lord said, "Hear what the unrighteous judge says. And will not God vindicate his elect, who cry to him day and night? Will he delay long over them? I tell you, he will vindicate them speedily. Nevertheless, when the Son of man comes, will he find faith on earth?" (Luke 18:1-8).

"And he told them a parable, to the effect that they ought always to pray and not lose heart." It was a most interesting parable, you must admit—a short one of only 146 words. There are two characters in the story. One is a judge, a man in a man's world. But he is not just any man; he is a man with power because he also has authority. The other person in the story is a widow. She is representative of the innocent, the powerless, and the oppressed. All she has going for her is her femaleness and her persistence, *but that is enough.* What she cannot accomplish because she has nothing that would influence the judge—such as money for a bribe, or special power in the community guaranteed by birth, marriage, or office—

she accomplishes with what seems useless: she uses her persistence. She can't even embarrass or shame the judge because he has no conscience, no regard whatsoever for another person.

If we did not have Luke's hint at the purpose of the parable, if it were left to us to decide what it was about, we might say it was a parable about justice denied and granted, or it might be a parable about patience and persistence, or it might be about not allowing ourselves to be unnecessarily intimidated by those who wield power over us.

But no! It was a parable to teach us that "we ought always to pray and not lose heart." It was a parable told to inspire confidence in praying. Who would have thought that? Jesus told it in order that we would grasp the importance of praying all the time, and that we should not despair in our praying. Every one of our prayers is heard and those that require answers are answered, though not necessarily to our immediate satisfaction.

As a companion to this parable, consider this modern true story. What follows is a simple but poignant exchange between two men from different worlds: one a sophisticated, highly skilled surgeon and the other a lowly, humble Italian monk. The vacationing surgeon went to the Abbey of San Giorgio Maggiore, where he was met by the guest master, Dom Pietro. The doctor clumsily carried his bags up the narrow winding staircase behind the monk who was all grace and figure in his flowing black habit.

At the door to the guest room, the monk stopped and offered the centuries-old greeting for welcoming each guest, "Enter, Christ."

The doctor replied, "Well, not exactly."

The monk ignored the doctor's remarks and apologized: "Four hundred years ago the abbot himself would have come to bathe your feet."

This time the doctor ignored the monk's comments as he asked, "How long have you been here?"

The terse explanation came without any lengthy thought or emotion but hung in the air like a helium-filled balloon, "We have been here one thousand years."[29]

In so stating his answer, the monk had dated the history of the monastery, but he had also stated in coded language, "We have been praying in this holy place for a thousand years."

The church of Christ has been praying for two thousand years and still we pray on. We, the church present, are the significant link between the church of the past and the church of the future. And as a people of prayer, we are the link between heaven and earth, between humanity and God. Our praying is our means of connecting. Perhaps this parable that Jesus told and this reflection from the lives of two men in an Italian monastery will remind you that the church "ought always to pray and not lose heart." And it would be better still if this parable from the Gospel of Luke and this real life story would inspire you to pray with confidence.

Now let us pray again—

> O God, you listen to so many strange prayers, so many good prayers. Prayers sobbed in frantic despair, and those stumbled through when we are deliriously happy. May we reach the point where our prayers will come to you with regularity. Lord, help us to pray our prayers and our lives with greater faithfulness, for Jesus' sake. Amen.

To think and talk through:

1. Have there been times in your life when you lost confidence in praying? Were these times of stress or times that some have labeled the "dark night of the soul" (a very unproductive period)?

2. Do you have a particular prayer you have prayed persistently for a long time? If not, if you were to fashion one for the future, what would it be?

3. Design a confidence scale or chart regarding your prayer life. Then position yourself on it. Is this where you want to be? If not, how might you work toward your desired position?

A Practicum for Individual and Group Prayer

Dunnam, Maxie, *The Workbook of Intercessory Prayer*. Nashville: The Upper Room, 1979.

Dunnam, Maxie, *The Workbook of Living Prayer*. Nashville: The Upper Room, 1974.

Intercessory Prayer

Bauman, Edward W., *Intercessory Prayer*. Philadelphia: The Westminster Press, 1968.

Cobb, John B. Jr., *Praying for Jennifer*. Nashville: The Upper Room, 1985.

RESOURCE LIST

Should you desire to read further about prayer, the following list is provided to help you in the task. This list is not meant to be comprehensive. Instead, consider it a sampler of some of the better books on the subject: some of which are anthologies, some are "how-to" books, and a few were written to help a person think through a theology of prayer.

A Collection of Prayers

Castle, Tony, compiler, *The New Book of Common Prayer.* New York: Crossroad, 1986.

Colquhoun, Frank, editor, *Parish Prayers.* London: Hodden & Stoughton, 1980, 8th impression.

Colquhoun, Frank, editor, *Contemporary Parish Prayers.* London: Hodden & Stoughton, 1980, 4th impression.

Colquhoun, Frank, editor, *New Parish Prayers.* London: Hodden & Stoughton, 1984, 3rd impression.

Shea, John, *The God Who Fell from Heaven.* Niles, Illinois: Argus Communications, 1979.

Suter, John Wallace, editor, *Prayers for a New World.* New York: Charles Scribner's Sons, 1964.

Williams, Dick, editor, *Prayers for Today's Church.* Minneapolis: Augsburg Publishing House, 1972.

14. C. S. Lewis, *The Screwtape Letters* (Old Tappan, NJ: Fleming H. Revell Company, 1976), p. 77.

15. John H. Townsend, March/April 1980 *Pulpit Digest,* p. (89) 17.

16. Carmen Bernos De Gasztold, tr. by Rumer Godden, *Prayers from the Ark* (New York: The Viking Press, 1973), p. 31.

17. *Interpreter's Dictionary of the Bible, Supplementary Volume* (Nashville: Abingdon Press, 1976), p. 73.

18. William O. Weldon, *Not Afraid! Thoughts on Fearless Living* (Nashville: The Upper Room, 1984), p. 57.

19. Robert A. Raines, *The Ridgeleaf* (an occasional paper from Kirkridge) (Bangor, PA, April 1987, #158).

20. Earl G. Hunt, Jr., *I Have Believed: A Bishop Talks about His Faith* (Nashville: The Upper Room, 1980), pp. 99-100.

21. W. H. Auden, "For the Time Being, A Christmas Oratorio," *The Collected Poetry of W. H. Auden* (New York: Random House, 1945), p. 457.

22. Theodore Roethke, *The Collected Poems of Theodore Roethke* (Garden City, NJ: Anchor Press/Doubleday, 1975), p. 130.

23. Richard Bimler, *Pray, Praise and Hooray* (St. Louis: Concordia Publishing House, 1972), p. 15.

24. Harry Emerson Fosdick, *The Meaning of Prayer* (New York: Association Press, 1949), p. 157.

25. Malcolm Muggeridge, *Something Beautiful for God* (New York: Harper and Row Pub., 1971), pp. 22 & 98.

26. C. S. Lewis, *The Screwtape Letters,* p. 125.

27. Henri J. Nouwen, *The Genesee Diary: Report from a Trappist Monastery* (Garden City, NJ: Doubleday & Co., 1976), p. 21.

28. James Baldwin, *Just Above My Head* (New York: Dell Publishing Co., 1980), p. 59.

29. Richard Selzer, *Taking the World in for Repairs* (New York: William Morrow & Co. Inc., 1986), p. 15.

NOTES

1. John Shea, *The God Who Fell from Heaven* (Niles, IL: Argus Communications, 1979), p. 7.

2. Douglas V. Steere, *Dimensions of Prayer* (New York: Women's Division Christian Service, Board of Missions, The Methodist Church, 1962), p. 6.

3. Ibid, p. 50.

4. Ibid, pp. 57-58.

5. Thanks to John Killinger and a sermon he preached to the people of the First Congregational Church of Los Angeles, Oct. 12, 1986, "How to Begin an Affair with God."

6. Herman C. Ahrens, Jr., *Tune-In* (Philadelphia: Pilgrim Press, 1969), p. 71.

7. Donald G. Bloesch, *The Struggle of Prayer* (New York: Harper & Row Pub., 1980), p. 73.

8. Ibid., p. 74.

9. Frederick Buechner, *Wishful Thinking: A Theological ABC* (New York: Harper & Row Pub., 1973), p. 70.

10. Richard Selzer, "Diary of an Infidel: Notes from a Monastery," *Taking the World in for Repairs* (New York: William Morrow & Co., 1986), pp. 336-337.

11. Ibid, p. 9.

12. Howard Thurman, *Deep Is the Hunger* (New York: Harper & Brothers, Inc., 1951), p. 158.

13. Madeleine L'Engle, *A Circle of Quiet* (New York: Farrar, Straus & Girauz, 1972), pp. 133-134.